Come to Jesus

A Kids' Book for Eucharistic Adoration

Sister Anne Flanagan, FSP

Pauline
BOOKS & MEDIA
Boston

Nihil Obstat:
Rev. Thomas W. Buckley

Imprimatur:
✠Most Rev. Seán O'Malley, O.F.M. Cap.
Archbishop of Boston
October 25, 2005

Cover photo by sidneydealmeida/Depositphotos

Illustrations by Janice Cleary

Special thanks to Sr. Fran Sulzer, FSPA, for insights into the human heart, and to Rev. Richard Fragomeni for his liturgical and pastoral perspectives.

ISBN 0-8198-1577-2

Published by Pauline Books & Media, 50 Saint Paul's Avenue, Boston, MA 02130-3491.

Printed in the U.S.A.

www.pauline.org

Pauline Books & Media is the publishing house of the Daughters of St. Paul, an international congregation of women religious serving the Church with the communications media.

3 4 5 6 7 8 9 10 11 25 24 23 22 21 20

Contents

About This Book

This book is yours for prayer before Jesus in the Eucharist. Each prayer outline is in three parts: Jesus our Truth, Jesus our Way, Jesus our Life. This matches what Jesus said, "I am the Way, the Truth, and the Life" (in the Bible, John 14:6). If you have a whole hour, about twenty minutes for each part will work out just right, but you can spend as much time as you want on each section. If you have a shorter amount of time, like ten minutes or so, try using one section. Then you can use the next section the next time you come for adoration.

Jesus welcomes you and says,

"Do not be afraid: I am with you!
From the Eucharist, my warm light shines
on you and all around you.
Keep your heart always open to my grace.
I love you!"

We Adore Jesus Who Promises Living Water

We Gather to Pray

At Sunday Mass, our whole parish family comes together. We hear God's Word and we join in Jesus' offering. Jesus even gives us his own Body as our Bread of Life! Now we come back to Jesus for more! We open our minds to God's message. We open our hearts to God's goodness. Our time of adoration helps us pray the Mass better.

Opening Prayer

I believe, my God, that you are here.
I love you!
You are great and holy.
I adore you!
You have given me every good thing I have.
Thank you very much!
I am happy to have this time with you.

Think about what you and Jesus are going to say to each other. Whom do you want to pray for? What blessings do you hope Jesus will send to the world through your prayer? How do you want to listen to Jesus today?

Prayer for Listening

I am so glad to be with you, Jesus! You are happy to welcome me here. You have words of everlasting life for me, and I want to listen. I give you all my worries and needs, so they do not stop me from hearing you. Please open my mind and my heart to your Holy Spirit.

Jesus Our Truth

Jesus teaches us. We welcome God's Word.

We are going to listen to God's Word in the Bible. First, let's picture the place. It is a town called Sychar. Sychar was a dry place. It hardly ever rained. The only water was deep underground. If you needed water, you had to get it with a bucket from the well. It was the only way. You could only get one bucket of water at a time. What a lot of work! And the water didn't even taste good! Can you imagine how important water must be for people in a town like Sychar?

A reading from the holy Gospel according to John (4:4–10, 15–19, 25–30, 39–42)

[This time] Jesus had to go through Samaria, and on his way he came to the town of Sychar. It was near the field that Jacob had long ago given to his son Joseph. The well that Jacob had dug was still there, and Jesus sat down beside it because he was tired from traveling. It was noon,

Janice

and after Jesus' disciples had gone into town to buy some food, a Samaritan woman came to draw water from the well. Jesus asked her, "Would you please give me a drink of water?"

"You are a Jew," she replied, "and I am a Samaritan woman. How can you ask me for a drink of water when Jews and Samaritans won't have anything to do with each other?"

Jesus answered, "You don't know what God wants to give you, and you don't know who is asking you for a drink. If you did, you would ask me for the water that gives life."

The woman replied, "Sir, please give me a drink of that water! Then I won't get thirsty and have to come to this well again."

Jesus told her, "Go and bring your husband."

The woman answered, "I don't have a husband."

"That's right," Jesus replied, "you're telling the truth. You don't have a husband. You have already been married five times, and the man you are now living with isn't your husband."

The woman said, "Sir, I can see that you are a prophet. I know that the Messiah will come. He is the one we call Christ. When he comes, he will explain everything to us."

"I am that one," Jesus told her, "and I am speaking to you now."

The disciples returned about this time and were surprised to find Jesus talking with a woman. But none of them asked him what he wanted or why he was talking to her.

The woman left her water jar and ran back into town. She said to the people, "Come and see a man who told me everything I have ever done! Could he be the Messiah?" Everyone in town went out to see Jesus.

A lot of Samaritans in that town put their faith in Jesus because the woman had said, "This man told me everything I have ever done." They came and asked him to stay in their town, and he stayed on for two days. Many more Samaritans put their faith in Jesus because of what they heard him say. They told the woman, "We no longer have faith in Jesus just because of what you told us. We have heard him ourselves, and we are certain that he is the Savior of the world!"

Quiet time with Jesus

There is an interesting thing about the woman who came to the well. Even though she tried to make people like her, she was unpopular in the town. So she came by herself to get water at the hottest, most awful time of the day.

When Jesus came to the well, he was tired and thirsty. He just couldn't take another step. When the lady came, Jesus could tell that nobody in town liked her. But that didn't matter to Jesus. He showed her respect. And he gave her a mission: Jesus told the woman who he really was. When she went back and told everyone about Jesus, they all came to him.

Jesus became like living water for the whole thirsty town. He brought them new life. They all said, "We believe that he is the Son of God!" And they thanked God for sending Jesus to their town.

My response

Imagine that you were in the town and heard the woman talk about Jesus. Would you go with everyone else to meet him? What would you tell Jesus there at the well? Tell him now. He is waiting to hear from you!

This is a good time to sing a song of faith!

OR

Act of Faith: **Jesus, we believe that you are the Son of God!**

Jesus Our Way

Jesus calls us. We choose to follow Jesus.

How good Jesus was to the woman at the well! She was sad and alone when she came, but after she met Jesus, she was happy. She was ready to tell the whole world that God's Son had come!

What is the best way to let people know about Jesus? By imitating him! Then people can see Jesus in us. Imitating Jesus means letting Jesus share his choices and his way of doing things with us.

How did Jesus live? By loving God and loving other people. This means treating other people the way we like to be treated.

Jesus knows we sometimes do mean and hurtful things. We don't always treat people the way we want to be treated. We can admit this to Jesus and tell him we are sorry.

Prayer of Repentance

Jesus, we come to you like the woman who came to the well. She had made many wrong choices in life, but you showed her a new way. We are sorry for the choices we have made that hurt other people. We love you and we want to treat other people the way we would treat you. You are full of goodness, so we know you want to bring us to happiness. Thank you, Jesus.

My response

Do you want to share in Jesus' way of making choices? Tell him, heart to heart. Ask Jesus to let you know how to make room for his way of making choices. (If you are not ready, that is okay. Tell Jesus that you do not feel ready. Ask him what he wants for you now.)

Quiet time with Jesus

Tell Jesus how you like others to treat you: at school, in games, in activities. Ask Jesus how he would like to be treated in those same places. He said, "Whatever you do to others, you do to me."

This is a good time to sing a song of hope!

OR

Act of Hope: **Jesus, you are our hope and our life!**
(Repeat this a few times, from your heart.)

Jesus Our Life

Jesus listens to us.
We open our hearts to pray and praise.

Litany of Praise

After each part of the prayer say:
We praise you for your glory!

We are glad God is so wonderful!
You gave us water for drinking and washing and playing!
You give the thirsty plants water to grow with!
You give our hearts the living water of your Spirit!
You want all of your children to be happy!

Mary was the best follower of Jesus ever. She can help us to look at Jesus, listen to him, love him, and follow him. The Rosary is one way we turn to Mary, asking her to show Jesus to us and keep us close to him. Pray one decade of the Rosary, thinking about the story of the Wedding at Cana:

The bride and groom at Cana didn't have enough wine to give their wedding guests a nice party. All they had left was water. Lots of water. Mary told Jesus, and Jesus turned the water into the best wine ever. He showed his glory that way. And his followers began to believe in him.

In Sychar, Jesus told the woman at the well his real plan: that people would burst with life—not from wells or water jars, but from the Holy Spirit. God wants us to come to know his love.

Intercessions

We STAND and pray for the needs of the whole world. After each part of the prayer say:

Hear our prayers for them, Lord.

God, there are people who do not have clean, healthy water to drink.

God, there are people who are sad and lonely.

God, there are people who do not know Jesus.

God, there are people who hurt others on purpose.

God, some people we know have big worries.

God, some people we know are sick. Their names are ____________________.

Now add your own prayers for other people and their needs.

We bring all our prayers of praise and petition together in the prayer that Jesus taught us. *Our Father…*

Quiet time with Jesus

Even though we cannot receive Jesus in Holy Communion right now, we can look forward to receiving Communion at Mass. Jesus wants to come into our hearts too! So let's share a moment of spiritual communion with Jesus. Let's be glad in his love and offer him our love.

Spiritual Communion Prayer

I want to unite my heart with yours, Jesus. I give you my gladness and my love and my hopes. I want to receive your own gladness and love in my heart.

This is a good time to sing a song of love and praise!

OR

Act of Love: **God, you want what is good for me. I love you!**

Closing Prayer

Thank you, God,
for giving us this special time with you.
Thank you for giving us your Word.
Thank you for listening to our prayers.
Thank you because you care about us all the time.
Jesus, fill us with your Holy Spirit.
Give us your Body as our Bread of Life when we go to Mass.
Make our thoughts just like yours so we can speak your words!
Make our choices just like yours so others can see how you lived!
Make our hearts just like yours so we can spread your love!

Lamb of God, you take away the sin of the world:
Grant us peace.

In the name of the Father,
and of the Son,
and of the Holy Spirit.
Amen.

We Go to Love and Serve!

We Adore Jesus with His First Followers

We Gather to Pray

At Sunday Mass, our whole parish family comes together. We hear God's Word and we join in Jesus' offering. Jesus even gives us his own Body as our Bread of Life! Now we come back to Jesus for more! We open our minds to God's message. We open our hearts to God's goodness. Our time of adoration helps us pray the Mass better.

Opening Prayer

I believe, my God, that you are here.
I love you!
You are great and holy.
I adore you!
You have given me every good thing I have.
Thank you very much!
I am happy to have this time with you.

Think about what you and Jesus are going to say to each other. Whom do you want to pray for? What blessings do you hope Jesus will send to the world through your prayer? How do you want to listen to Jesus today?

Prayer for Listening

I am so glad to be with you, Jesus! You are happy to welcome me here. You have words of everlasting life for me, and I want to listen. I give you all my worries and needs, so they do not stop me from hearing you. Please open my mind and my heart to your Holy Spirit.

Jesus Our Truth

Jesus teaches us. We welcome God's Word.

We are going to listen to God's Word in the Bible. First, let's picture the place.

It's a green place with trees and water and people... By the water is a man. His name is John. People are listening to John because he's telling them about God. Jesus is just walking by. In your imagination, run over to where he is. Jesus welcomes you with a big smile. Then you hear John's voice say, "Look! Here is the Lamb of God who takes away the sins of the world!"

A reading from the holy Gospel according to John (1:35–48)

The next day, John was there again, and two of his followers were with him. When he saw Jesus walking by, he said, "Here is the Lamb of God!" John's two followers heard him, and they went with Jesus

When Jesus turned and saw them, he asked, "What do

Janice

you want?" They answered, "Rabbi, where do you live?" The Hebrew word "Rabbi" means "Teacher."

Jesus replied, "Come and see!" It was already about four o'clock in the afternoon when they went with him and saw where he lived. So they stayed on for the rest of the day.

One of the two men who had heard John and had gone with Jesus was Andrew, the brother of Simon Peter. The first thing Andrew did was to find his brother and tell him, "We have found the Messiah!" The Hebrew word "Messiah" means the same as the Greek word "Christ."

Andrew brought his brother to Jesus. And when Jesus saw him, he said, "Simon son of John, you will be called Cephas." This name can be translated as "Peter."

The next day Jesus decided to go to Galilee. There he met Philip, who was from Bethsaida, the hometown of Andrew and Peter. Jesus said to Philip, "Come with me."

Philip then found Nathanael and said, "We have found the one that Moses and the Prophets wrote about. He is Jesus, the son of Joseph from Nazareth."

Nathanael asked, "Can anything good come from Nazareth?"

Philip answered, "Come and see."

When Jesus saw Nathanael coming toward him, he said, "Here is a true descendant of our ancestor Israel. And he isn't deceitful."

"How do you know me?" Nathanael asked.

Jesus answered, "Before Philip called you, I saw you under the fig tree."

Quiet time with Jesus

John the Baptizer was a real hero. Even though everyone thought he was special and important, he did not say, "Look at me!" Instead, he told them, "Look at Jesus: he is the real Lamb of God. He takes away sin and evil and hurt." Jesus said that John was one of the greatest people alive, but that when we become God's children, we are even greater.

Jesus, thank you for taking away the sin of the world!
Jesus, thank you for making us children of God!

My response

Imagine that you saw Andrew and the other person coming to follow Jesus. What would you tell them about Jesus?

This is a good time to sing a song of faith!

OR

Act of Faith, which can be repeated three times (standing):
Jesus, we believe that you are the One God promised to send!

Jesus Our Way

Jesus calls us. We choose to follow Jesus.

We can all be like John: we can point to Jesus. We can be like Andrew: we can tell people about Jesus. We can be like Philip and bring people to Jesus. What would have happened if John had been silent? Or if Andrew hadn't gone to get his brother Peter? Or if Philip just left Nathaniel there under the tree?

John and Andrew and Philip all said good things to their friends. In fact, there was a lot of talking going on between those friends of Jesus. Talking is a wonderful gift! When we talk, other people can find out what is inside of our minds and hearts. Without talking, we cannot really know people too well.

Thank you, God, for words!
Thank you, God, for our voices!
Thank you, God, for jokes and songs and nicknames and books!
Thank you, God, that we can talk and sing!

Sometimes, we misuse the gift of talking. We tell lies and say mean things. Or else we stay quiet when it is really important to tell a grown-up something that is happening to us or to a friend.

Prayer of repentance

Jesus, lies and mean words come from sin and they lead to sin. We are sorry for the lies we have told. We are sorry for the mean things we have said to each other. We are sorry for hiding the truth. You are the Lamb of God who takes away all the sin of the world. Take away our lies and mean words. Guide our choices in the truth. Make us brave and strong in the truth.

My response

Talk with Jesus about how you want to use your gift of speech. Ask him to help you to say what is good and true and helpful, the way John and Andrew and Peter did.

Quiet time with Jesus

Many times when we are afraid, we tell lies or say mean things. Tell Jesus about the things you are afraid of. Listen to him say to you, "Do not be afraid: I am with you." And if he tells you to let a grown-up you feel safe with know about what scares you, be sure to listen.

This is a good time to sing a song of hope!

OR

Act of Hope: **Jesus, you will always be near me.**

We Give God Thanks and Praise

Jesus Our Life

Jesus listens to us.
We open our hearts to pray and praise.

Litany of Praise

After each part of the prayer say:
We worship you! We give you thanks!

We are glad God is so wonderful!
God, you inspired John to recognize your Son, Jesus!
God, you inspired Andrew to tell his brother about Jesus!

God, you gave us family and teachers who told us about Jesus!

God, you gave us a Pope who serves us like Jesus!

God, you gave us books and websites and songs that tell about Jesus!

Mary was the best follower of Jesus ever. She can help us to look at Jesus, listen to him, love him, and follow him. The Rosary is one way we turn to Mary, asking her to show Jesus to us and keep us close to him. Pray one decade of the Rosary, thinking about the story of the Baptism of the Lord:

Before Jesus started his mission, John was telling people to change their lives and get ready for God. Then Jesus came. He wanted John to baptize him! John tried to say no, but Jesus told him it was part of God's plan. And so John brought Jesus into the water. Then a voice called out from the sky, "This is my beloved Son. I am so pleased with him." John knew that God had come to save his people.

Intercessions

We STAND and pray for the needs of the world. After each part of the prayer say:

Hear our prayers for them, Lord.

God, there are people who have been treated unfairly.

God, there are people who can't find a job.

God, there are people who are waiting for Jesus.

God, there are people whom Jesus is calling to follow him in a special way.

God, some people we know are worried.
God, some people we know are sick. Their names are ____________________.

Now add your own prayers for other people and their needs.

We bring all our prayers of praise and petition together in the prayer Jesus taught us. *Our Father…*

Quiet time with Jesus

Even though we cannot receive Jesus in Holy Communion right now, we can look forward to receiving Communion at Mass. Jesus wants to come into our hearts too! So let's share a moment of spiritual communion with Jesus. Let's be glad in his love and offer him our love.

Spiritual Communion Prayer

I want to unite my heart with yours, Jesus. I give you my gladness and my love and my hopes. I want to receive your own gladness and love in my heart.

This is a good time to sing a song of love and praise!
OR
Act of Love: **God, I love you and I count on you.**

Closing Prayer

Thank you, God,
for giving us this special time with you.
Thank you for giving us your Word.

Thank you for listening to our prayers.
Thank you because you care about us all the time.
Jesus, fill us with your Holy Spirit.
Give us your Body as our Bread of Life when we go to Mass.
Make our thoughts just like yours so we can speak your words!
Make our choices just like yours so others can see how you lived!
Make our hearts just like yours so we can spread your love!

Lamb of God, you take away the sin of the world:
Grant us peace.

In the name of the Father,
and of the Son,
and of the Holy Spirit.
Amen.

We Go to Love and Serve!

We Adore Jesus Who Gives Us What Is Good

We Gather to Pray

At Sunday Mass, our whole parish family comes together. We hear God's Word and we join in Jesus' offering. Jesus even gives us his own Body as our Bread of Life!

Now we come back to Jesus for more! We open our minds to God's message. We open our hearts to God's goodness. Our time of adoration helps us pray the Mass better.

Opening Prayer

I believe, my God, that you are here.
I love you!
You are great and holy.
I adore you!
You have given me every good thing I have.
Thank you very much!
I am happy to have this time with you.

Think about what you and Jesus are going to say to each other. Whom do you want to pray for? What blessings do you hope Jesus will send to the world through your prayer? How do you want to listen to Jesus today?

Prayer for Listening

I am so glad to be with you, Jesus! You are happy to welcome me here. You have words of everlasting life for me, and I want to listen. I give you all my worries and needs, so they do not stop me from hearing you. Please open my mind and my heart to your Holy Spirit.

Jesus Our Truth

Jesus teaches us. We welcome God's Word.

We are going to listen to God's Word in the Bible. First, let's picture the place.

Imagine a grassy hill overlooking a big blue lake. Thousands and thousands of people are there. They are waiting for Jesus. He is coming across the lake in a boat. Everyone wants to be with Jesus.

A reading from the holy Gospel according to John (6:1–13)

Jesus crossed Lake Galilee, which was also known as Lake Tiberias. A large crowd had seen him work miracles to heal the sick, and those people went with him. It was almost time for the Jewish festival of Passover, and Jesus went up on a mountain with his disciples and sat down.

When Jesus saw the large crowd coming toward him, he asked Philip, "Where will we get enough food to feed all these people?" He said this to test Philip, since he already knew what he was going to do.

Philip answered, "Don't you know that it would take almost a year's wages just to buy only a little bread for each of these people?"

Andrew, the brother of Simon Peter, was one of the disciples. He spoke up and said, "There is a boy here who has five small loaves of barley bread and two fish. But what good is that with all these people?"

The ground was covered with grass, and Jesus told his disciples to have everyone sit down. About five thousand men were in the crowd. Jesus took the bread in his hands and gave thanks to God. Then he passed the bread to the people, and he did the same with the fish, until everyone had plenty to eat.

The people ate all they wanted, and Jesus told his disciples to gather up the leftovers, so that nothing would be wasted. The disciples gathered them up and filled twelve large baskets with what was left over from the five barley loaves.

Quiet time with Jesus

When you heard the Bible story, which words did your heart hear the loudest? Let them stay in your heart. Repeat them quietly. Look at the picture in this book or in your own imagination. Where is Jesus? Where are you? What is Jesus suggesting to you? How do you want to answer him?

My response

What would you tell Jesus if you were the child who had the bread and fish?

Everything we have is really from God, even when it comes through people. Instead of bread and fish, what are the good things you have from God? (Remember your talents, like being a good reader, or playing a musical instrument, or being a great team player: these are gifts from God, too!) What good things can you do for the world with your special gifts? Tell Jesus about it now!

This is a good time to sing a song of faith!

OR

Act of Faith: **Jesus, we are sure that you are good.**

Jesus Our Way

Jesus calls us. We choose to follow Jesus.

Those five thousand men and their families probably didn't know it, but they had dinner with Jesus because one little child was willing to share. The crowd could only see the miracle Jesus did with the child's gift, but Jesus knew where his miracle had started: with a child's sharing.

Jesus shared, too. He was as tired and hungry as the others were, but he gave the people his time, his message, and his miracle. In the Eucharist, Jesus shares his entire self with us!

What are some things that people have shared with you?

My response

Talk to Jesus about the kinds of choices you make when it comes to sharing. What makes sharing hard for you? What do you usually do when you see that there may not be as much of a good thing as you want for yourself? If you remember times when you were selfish or greedy, give that memory to Jesus.

Ask Jesus to teach you how to give and to receive what is good, as he did.

Prayer of Repentance

Jesus, when we refuse to share, we are making things more important than people. So much unhappiness comes from that! We are sorry for the choices we have made to take and keep things that are meant for everybody. When it is time to share, show us how to do it. Thank you for giving us everything we have! Jesus, live in us with your own way of sharing.

Quiet time with Jesus

The Bible says, "There is more happiness in giving than in receiving" (see Acts 20:35). Does that make you stop and think? Giving and receiving are both very important! Imagine being at a big table with hundreds of people. Everyone has a bowl of delicious soup, but no one is able to eat it because the spoons are as long as broomsticks! Then one child lifts a spoonful of soup across the table to a younger child, and the little one offers a spoonful of soup back. Before long, everyone is enjoying a wonderful meal. What made the difference?

Ask Jesus to help you understand the secret happiness of sharing.

This is a good time to sing a song of hope!

OR

Act of Hope: **Jesus, you will take care of everything we need.**

We Give God Thanks and Praise

Jesus Our Life

Jesus listens to us.
We open our hearts to pray and praise.

Litany of Praise

After each part of the prayer say:
It is right to give you thanks and praise!

We are glad God is so wonderful!
God, you made the earth and everything in it!
God, you made all people one family!
God, you shared your own Son with us!
God, you share your own life with us!
God, you want everyone to be happy!

Mary was the best follower of Jesus ever. She can help us to look at Jesus, listen to him, love him, and follow him. The Rosary is one way we turn to Mary, asking her to show Jesus to us and keep us close to him. Pray one decade of the Rosary, thinking about the story of the Last Supper, when Jesus gave us the Eucharist.

When Jesus gave the people on the hillside the miracle of fish and bread to eat, he was preparing them to receive the great gift of the Eucharist, the Bread of Life. Jesus gave us the Eucharist when he had dinner with his friends before he died for us. Jesus wanted us to remember him. He took bread and said, "Eat this, it is my body which is given for you." And he took wine and said, "Drink this, it is my blood which is poured out for you."

He told us to do these things in his memory. At Mass, we do what Jesus said to do, and then we are sent out to share God's Word with everyone else.

Intercessions

We STAND and pray for the needs of the world. After each part of the prayer say:

Hear our prayers for them, Lord.

God, there are people who are hungry all the time.

God, there are people who do not have a place to live.

God, there are people who do not have anyone to take care of them.

God, there are people who have more than they need, but who do not want to share.

God, there are people who cheat others just to have more for themselves.

God, some people we know asked us to pray for them.

God, some people we know are sick. Their names are ____________________.

Now add your own prayers for other people and their needs.

We bring all our prayers of praise and petition together into the prayer Jesus taught us. *Our Father...*

Quiet time with Jesus

Even though we cannot receive Jesus in Holy Communion right now, we can look forward to receiving Communion at Mass. Jesus wants to come into our hearts too! So let's share a moment of spiritual communion with Jesus. Let's be glad in his love and offer him our love.

Spiritual Communion Prayer

I want to unite my heart with yours, Jesus. I give you my gladness and my love and my hopes. I want to receive your own gladness and love in my heart.

This is a good time to sing a song of love and praise!
OR
Act of Love: **God, I love you and I thank you for everything.**

Closing Prayer

Thank you, God,
for giving us this special time with you.
Thank you for giving us your Word.
Thank you for listening to our prayers.
Thank you because you care about us all the time.
Jesus, fill us with your Holy Spirit.
Give us your Body as our Bread of Life when we go to Mass.

Make our thoughts just like yours so we can speak your words!
Make our choices just like yours so others can see how you lived!
Make our hearts just like yours so we can spread your love!

Lamb of God, you take away the sin of the world:
Grant us peace.

In the name of the Father,
and of the Son,
and of the Holy Spirit.
Amen.

We Go to Love and Serve!

Some Basic Prayers

The Sign of the Cross

In the name of the Father, and of the Son, and of the Holy Spirit. Amen.

Our Father

Our Father, who art in heaven, hallowed be thy name. Thy kingdom come. Thy will be done on earth as it is in heaven. Give us this day our daily bread, and forgive us our trespasses, as we forgive those who trespass against us. And lead us not into temptation; but deliver us from evil. Amen.

Hail Mary

Hail Mary, full of grace, the Lord is with you. Blessed are you among women and blessed is the fruit of your womb, Jesus. Holy Mary, Mother of God, pray for us sinners, now and at the hour of our death. Amen.

Glory

Glory to the Father, and to the Son, and to the Holy Spirit: as it was in the beginning, is now, and will be for ever. Amen.

The Apostles' Creed

I believe in God, the Father almighty,
creator of heaven and earth.

I believe in Jesus Christ, his only Son, our Lord.
He was conceived by the power of the Holy Spirit
and born of the Virgin Mary.
He suffered under Pontius Pilate,
was crucified, died and was buried.
He descended to the dead.
On the third day he rose again.
He ascended into heaven,
and is seated at the right hand of the Father.
He will come again to judge the living and the dead.

I believe in the Holy Spirit,
the holy catholic Church,
the communion of saints,
the forgiveness of sins,
the resurrection of the body,
and the life everlasting. Amen.

Hail, Holy Queen

Hail, holy Queen, Mother of Mercy, our life, our sweetness, and our hope. To you do we cry, poor banished children of Eve; to you do we send up our sighs, mourning and weeping in this valley of tears. Turn then, most gracious advocate, your eyes of mercy toward us, and after this our exile, show unto us the blessed fruit of your womb, Jesus. O clement, O loving, O sweet Virgin Mary.

The Rosary

The Rosary is a prayer that helps us remember the lives of Jesus and Mary. While we think about Jesus and Mary, we pray the Our Father, the Hail Mary, and the Glory. We use a chain of beads called rosary beads. The mysteries of the Rosary are different events from the lives of Jesus and Mary. We pray with four different sets of mysteries. Each set has its own name. There are the joyful mysteries. There are the mysteries of light. There are the sorrowful mysteries. And there are the glorious mysteries. We think about one set of mysteries every time we pray the Rosary.

The Joyful Mysteries

1. The Annunciation—Mary becomes the Mother of God
2. The Visitation—Mary visits Elizabeth
3. The Nativity—Jesus is born in a stable in Bethlehem
4. The Presentation of Jesus in the Temple—Mary and Joseph present Jesus to God
5. The Finding of Jesus in the Temple—Mary and Joseph find Jesus talking about God his Father

The Mysteries of Light

1. The Baptism of Jesus—John baptizes Jesus
2. The Wedding at Cana—Jesus works his first miracle
3. Jesus Announces God's Kingdom—Jesus teaches the people to turn their hearts to God

4. The Transfiguration—Jesus shines with the glory of God
5. Jesus Gives Us the Holy Eucharist—Jesus offers us his Body and Blood as food to make us strong in love and holiness

The Sorrowful Mysteries

1. The Agony in the Garden—Jesus suffers and prays
2. The Scourging at the Pillar—Jesus is tied up and whipped
3. The Crowning with Thorns—The soldiers make fun of Jesus
4. The Carrying of the Cross—Jesus carries his heavy cross
5. The Crucifixion—Jesus is nailed to the cross and dies for us

The Glorious Mysteries

1. The Resurrection—Jesus rises from the dead
2. The Ascension—Jesus goes back to heaven
3. The Descent of the Holy Spirit—the Holy Spirit comes down upon Mary and the apostles
4. The Assumption—Mary is taken body and soul to heaven
5. The Coronation—Mary is crowned queen of heaven and earth

1. Make the **Sign of the Cross** and pray the **Apostles' Creed**.
2. Pray the **Our Father**.
3. Pray 3 **Hail Marys**.
4. Pray the **Glory**, name the first mystery, and pray the **Our Father**.
5. Pray 10 **Hail Marys**.
6. Pray the **Glory**, name the second mystery, and pray the **Our Father**.
7. Repeat steps 5 and 6 until you reach the end.
8. Pray the **Glory** and the **Hail, Holy Queen**. Kiss the crucifix.

Notes for Adult Prayer Leaders

Thank you for your willingness to share the treasure of Eucharistic spirituality with children!

Since the Eucharist is the "whole spiritual treasure of the Church," no better introduction to Catholic prayer can be offered to the young than Eucharistic Adoration. Eucharistic spirituality is also the key to evangelization, our prime mission as Catholics. At Mass, we are fed by the Word of God and the Bread of Life, and then, transformed by these powerful gifts, we are sent into our everyday milieu. Wherever we go, we become extensions of Jesus' presence, bringing God's Word and the living presence of Jesus into all our relationships, conversations, decisions. When we return to Mass on Sunday, we do not come alone: we bring to the Eucharistic celebration everyone we met or dealt with during the week. Ideally, those who have encountered Christ in and through us will themselves be led to the Eucharist, to receive the Word of God and the Body of Christ, and to be sent in communion with the whole Church to evangelize.

Our prayer in Eucharistic Adoration is intimately associated with our participation in the Mass. From the early years of the Church, the Eucharist has been reserved for the sick who cannot join the assembly for the Eucharistic celebration. The Eucharist we adore comes from the Mass, and our adoration leads us back to Mass and Eucharistic Communion.

Adoration equips us for an even more effective evangelizing mission.

The Daughters of St. Paul, publishers of this book, have a profoundly apostolic Eucharistic spirituality that is their heritage from their Founder, Blessed James Alberione.

Blessed Alberione proposed a three-fold pattern for the Hour of Adoration that members of the Pauline Family pray daily. The method brings the "whole" person into adoration: the heart or the feelings, but also the mind, the will, and the conscious values and choices that determine the flow of our day. All are brought into contact with Jesus, the Way, the Truth, and the Life. We meet Jesus Truth especially through the Word of God in the Bible, although at times your own scriptural reading may be accompanied by documents of the Church, writings of outstanding theologians, and the examples of the saints. Jesus Way is our model and guide: we take his examples and teachings from the Gospel and let them speak to our daily choices, unafraid of the call to deeper conversion. Jesus Life gives us the gift of praise and intercession, as we turn to him in the prayer of the heart. And so the whole person, mind, will, and heart, meets the whole Christ, Way, Truth, and Life. The Way, Truth, and Life pattern is adopted for this book, but subheadings representing the principal parts of the Mass have also been included as a way of indicating that the Eucharistic celebration is the source and goal of our adoration. (These subheadings are in gray type.)

Practical Recommendations for Using This Book with Groups

The three prayer outlines offered here are suitable for half-hour to one-hour periods of time, but the method can be adapted for shorter periods. The book is a "tutorial" more than a prayer book. Its aim is to help children develop a life of prayer in which they encounter Jesus on a variety of levels, including the level of imagination. What we do (and how we do it) teaches much more effectively than what we might say. Our words can easily be lost, but gestures, habits, and attitudes enter in and form a kind of substructure on which convictions can grow. It is natural to want to take advantage of this time with the children for the purpose of teaching them, but in adoration, it is Jesus who is the teacher: we are all disciples who "come to him" and "learn from him" (see Mt 11:28–30). This is his time to speak, so don't be afraid of silence! Some very soft instrumental music may be useful, however, especially if something happens to trigger a case of the giggles.

Children should be given places that make it easy for them to see the tabernacle or (if the Blessed Sacrament is exposed) the altar. The children should not be too close together: each child needs room to move and gesture freely without bumping into someone else.

It is better that children not be given "parts" to lead or read aloud. If the prayer time resembles a school activity the children would be more naturally inclined to slip into their habitual school roles (dutiful student, class clown, etc.). Instead, let the prayer be directed by one or two adults who are positioned behind the children. The adult "presence" should be limited to a voice: the grown-ups should barely be noticed. With very small children, a grown-up with a non-speaking part could be toward the front (but not directly in front of the Blessed Sacrament) to model gestures and postures of adoration (bow), intercession (hands chest high, palms up), openness (palms open in the lap), and praise (hands at shoulder height, fingers pointing outward, palms facing front or slightly tilted upward).

While the leader's voice should be loud enough to be heard, it should not be overwhelming. The tone must still be gentle, warm, slow, contemplative. If you have access to a microphone, use it; it will allow you to speak very softly while still being heard.

The amplification will also make your voice and breath sound very near, creating an atmosphere of deeper intimacy with God, who first breathed the Spirit into us. Read slowly, softly, deliberately, with warm enthusiasm rather than with excitement. Pause frequently to allow for contemplative resonance in the children's souls—and in your own.

Naturally, adoration of the Eucharist does not require exposition of the Blessed Sacrament. The Eucharist is to be adored whether reserved in the tabernacle or exposed for veneration. In either case, if the children are entering a Blessed Sacrament chapel, a simple genuflection on one knee is appropriate before they go to their places. More elaborate gestures are not in conformity with the

Church's liturgical norms and would be out of place. If the children are assembled in another place for prayer, it is fitting for them to kneel when the Blessed Sacrament is brought in for adoration.

If the children can tolerate incense, its use can contribute to the "body-prayer" dimension. Children can see their own prayers "rise like incense" before the Lord, and "fill the temple" with the perfume of grace. Check with parents for concerns about asthma or allergies.

For the encounter with Jesus-Truth in the Word, a procession with the Bible could underline the relationship between Word and Eucharist. The children can follow the child who holds the Bible high; this intensifies their bodily participation in adoration.

The prayers may be recited all together or prayed one line at a time, first by the leader and then repeated by the group—whichever approach helps the children to pray with greater focus.

The opening song of each prayer time can be a version of Psalm 100 ("We are God's people") or another song the children know which combines recognition of God's presence with delight in God. The closing song is most appropriately a song of thanksgiving.

More ideas for using this book, particularly in a classroom setting, can be found on the Internet at www.pauline.org.

May our Eucharistic Lord bless you with a sharing in his own spirit of adoration and praise!

"I thank you, Father, Lord of Heaven and earth, for what you have hidden from the learned and the clever, you have revealed to the little ones" (Mt 11:25).

Eucharistic Adoration Resources

For Children

The Holy Eucharist Coloring & Activity Book, D. Thomas Halpin, FSP, and Virginia Helen Richards, FSP, Pauline Books & Media.

Jesus with Us: The Gift of the Eucharist, Anthony Tarzia, Pauline Books & Media.

My Book of Prayers, compiled by the Daughters of St. Paul, Pauline Books & Media.

Anna Goes to a Party and Learns About the Mass, Gabriele Kramer-Kost, Pauline Books & Media.

The Mass Explained for Kids, Maria Grace Dateno, FSP, Pauline Books & Media.

For Adults

Life for the World: A Way of Eucharistic Adoration for Today, Marie Paul Curley, FSP, Pauline Books & Media.

On the Eucharist in Its Relationship to the Church, Pope John Paul II, Pauline Books & Media.

Prayers for Eucharistic Adoration, Marie Paul Curley, FSP, Pauline Books & Media.

Reflections and Prayers for Visits with Our Eucharistic Lord, John Cardinal Carberry, Pauline Books & Media.

The Mass Explained, Maria Grace Dateno, FSP, Pauline Books & Media.

DVD's

Eucharist: A Journey of Transformation, Healing, and Discipleship, Dr. Mary Amore, Pauline Books & Media.

Eucharistic Adoration: Love, Mercy, and Friendship with Jesus, Dr. Mary Amore, Pauline Books & Media.

Pauline
BOOKS & MEDIA

The Daughters of St. Paul operate book and media centers at the following addresses. Visit, call, or write the one nearest you today, or find us at www.paulinestore.org.

CALIFORNIA
3908 Sepulveda Blvd, Culver City, CA 90230 — 310-397-8676
3250 Middlefield Road, Menlo Park, CA 94025 — 650-562-7060

FLORIDA
145 SW 107th Avenue, Miami, FL 33174 — 305-559-6715

HAWAII
1143 Bishop Street, Honolulu, HI 96813 — 808-521-2731

ILLINOIS
172 North Michigan Avenue, Chicago, IL 60601 — 312-346-4228

LOUISIANA
4403 Veterans Memorial Blvd, Metairie, LA 70006 — 504-887-7631

MASSACHUSETTS
885 Providence Hwy, Dedham, MA 02026 — 781-326-5385

MISSOURI
9804 Watson Road, St. Louis, MO 63126 — 314-965-3512

NEW YORK
115 E. 29th Street, New York City, NY 10016 — 212-754-1110

SOUTH CAROLINA
243 King Street, Charleston, SC 29401 — 843-577-0175

VIRGINIA
1025 King Street, Alexandria, VA 22314 — 703-549-3806

CANADA
3022 Dufferin Street, Toronto, ON M6B 3T5 — 416-781-9131